D1322839

GRACE DARLING

The Heroine of the Farne Islands

by Christine Bell ~ illustrated by Ruth Bayley

Christine Bell
07/04/04
Ruth Bayley

is especially presented to Miss Ellen Sarah Steiner of Rogart, Meadvale ~ by the Author and Illustrator

FOR GUY AND HONOR

Bamburgh Castle stands high on the rocks, on the North East Coast of Northumberland, where it towers majestically over land and sea.

Way below the Castle, snuggled beneath the sheer, ivy covered rocks, where the great grey and white Fulmers nest in the Spring, and sheltered from the strong blustery winds that howl around the coast, lies the little village of Bamburgh.

It was here, on the 24th November 1815,
that Grace Darling was born in the home of
her grandfather, Job Horsley.

When she was just three weeks old she was christened
in St. Aidan's Church, which stands across the road
from the cottage. She was named Grace Horsley Darling,
in memory of her grandmother, who had died
the previous year.

Grace was then taken home across the water to the
Farne Islands, where her father William Darling
was the Lightkeeper.

Their home was a cottage on Brownsman Island, which lies in the middle of the group of twenty eight islands called The Farnes, about two miles off the coast from Bamburgh Castle.

The islands are very wild and desolate places. The rough sea crashes over them, and the strong, blustery winds howl around their shores. Many of the islands are hidden beneath the water, for the tides are exceptionally high at times.

No trees grow on the islands, but they are inhabited by thousands of sea birds, which swoop and dive and zoom across the water at terrific speed, filling the air with their piercing cries.

There are Terns or sea swallows, beautiful birds,
which dive aggressively to protect their nests hidden
in the coarse grass.
There are Guillemots, Razor Bills and Kittiwakes which jostle for
space on the steep, rocky ledges to lay their eggs.

The Herring Gulls are the noisiest of birds. They soar
over the islands waiting their opportunity to steal eggs and
nestlings from the other birds. There are Black Headed Gulls
and Lesser Black Backed Gulls too.
Some of the rocks are covered with limewash and partly
digested fish, and as you approach the islands the pungent
smell meets you. These are the breeding grounds of the Shags
and Cormorants. They build their nests with piles of seaweed.
They are excellent fishermen, often catching over six kilo's of
fish a day, which they swallow whole. When they come out of
the water they often stand with their wings outstretched drying
their feathers in the breeze.

The most comical of the birds are the Puffins, sometimes
called Sea Parrots because of their brightly coloured
bills. They dig a deep burrow in the ground,
using their bills to loosen the soil and
their webbed feet to shovel it.
Then they lay one large egg in a
chamber at the end of the tunnel.

It was here, on Brownsman, amongst the birds and wild flowers that covered the island, and surrounded by the wild North Sea, that William and Thomasin Darling raised their family.

Grace was the seventh child. She had five brothers and three sisters, and a pet dog called Happy.

All the children were given family names.

Her eldest brother William, born in 1806, was named after his father. Then came twin girls in 1808, Thomasin, named after her mother, and Mary Ann, named after an aunt. Job came next in 1810. He was given Grandfather Horsley's name. Elizabeth Grace, born in 1812, was number five, and named after Grandma Darling. Robert named after Grandfather Darling followed in 1814. Then came Grace, named Grace Horsley Darling after Grandma Horsley. After Grace, twin boys were born in 1819. They were named George Alexander after Great Grandfather Darling, and William Brooks after a Great Uncle.

Having three Williams in the house must have been quite confusing at times. Their little cottage was very crowded, but they were a very happy and contented family.

William

Thomasin

Mary Ann

Job

Elizabeth Grace

Robert

Grace Horsley

George Alexander
William Brooks

When the children were small they played happily
together on the island among the flowers and the birds.
When she was really busy Mrs Darling often tethered
them as they played so that they wouldn't fall from the
slippery rocks into the sea.

Grace liked to pick the pretty pink Thrift and the Sea
Campion that grew around the cottage. She made friends
with the Eider Ducks that waddled about, and they didn't
mind when she stroked them as they sat on their nests.
When the Eiders had taken their ducklings to the sea the
Darling children would collect the soft downy feathers
from their nests. These were used to make pillows and
quilts for the family.

As they grew up Mr. Darling taught them how to read and write. He taught them local folksongs too, which they sang heartily as he accompanied them on his violin. They learned how to fish and how to row their boat, a large, sturdy, Northumberland coble that needed three people at the oars.

The children loved to be out on the water. They laughed at the inquisitive grey seals that popped their heads out of the water to look at them. These creatures are so streamlined and graceful in the sea, but on the rocks where they rest, they are awkward and clumsy, flopping about with giant caterpillar like movements.
The children learned the names of the fish and all the other sea creatures that lived in the waters around the Farnes. They could name the birds and flowers. They knew about other countries and where the passing ships came from, and where they were going. They learned about the history of England, and most important to them they studied the Bible, and because they couldn't get across to church each Sunday Mr. Darling read sermons to them and they said their prayers together.

The children had to work very hard. They all had their tasks to do to keep the lighthouse running smoothly and efficiently. Mr. Darling was paid £70 a year by Trinity House to look after the lighthouse, but the rest of the family were not paid, even though they all had to do their share of the work. Their reward was being allowed to live with him on the island.

As a family they had to be self-sufficient. Mrs. Darling taught the children how to cook, spin, weave and sew.

They helped to look after the goats which they kept for milk, and the sheep which provided them with meat and wool. They made a garden where they grew vegetables, though often the treacherous currents, racing tides and gale force winds swept everything away and they had to start all over again. As fish was a main source of food, they went fishing every day, and if they had a large catch it was salted and dried and kept for the winter. The children collected eggs for breakfast and Mr. Darling often used his gun to supply birds for their table. Other necessary supplies which they could not get for themselves, like tea, sugar, flour, bacon and most important of all, fresh water, were brought from the mainland in the supply ship.

Their hardest and most important task was the maintenance of the light, which had to be kept burning twenty four hours a day to warn the passing ships of the dangerous rocks.

The first lighthouse on Brownsman Island was built in 1795,and Grace's Grandfather, Robert Darling, was the Lightkeeper. It was a square tower, by the side of the cottage, standing about thirteen metres high, and the light was provided by a coal and timber fire. This was very unsatisfactory, as the winds and storms often put the fire out when it was most needed. The Darling family must have found this very tiresome.

In 1810 a second lighthouse was built at the other side of the cottage. It had a revolving light with silvered copper reflectors, and oil was used instead of coal. This was a big improvement. William Darling succeeded his father as Lightkeeper in 1815, the year in which Grace was born.

In those days the sea was a very busy place. Many vessels passed by the Farne Islands, sailing in the sheltered, less hazardous channel, called the Fairway, between the Inner Farne and the mainland where it was free from submerged rocks. However in the early 1800's engines were being invented, and larger, heavier ships were appearing on the sea. These ships could not travel along the Fairway as the water was too shallow. They had to go out into deeper water. The sailors navigating the ships had to look for the Brownsman light and go further out, but many were not going out far enough and were wrecked on the dangerous rocks of the Outer Farnes.

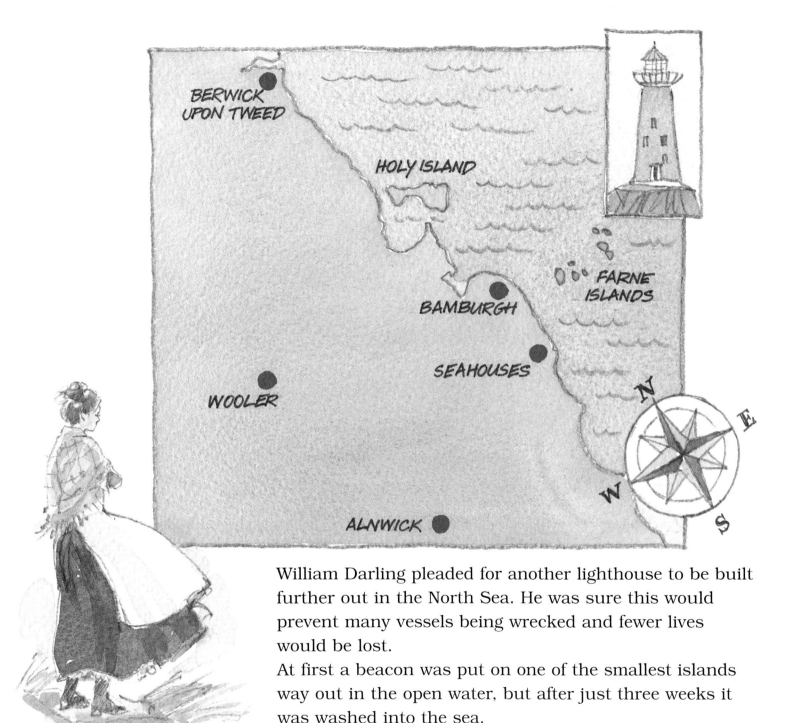

William Darling pleaded for another lighthouse to be built further out in the North Sea. He was sure this would prevent many vessels being wrecked and fewer lives would be lost.

At first a beacon was put on one of the smallest islands way out in the open water, but after just three weeks it was washed into the sea.

In 1825 Trinity House commissioned a new lighthouse to be built on Longstone Island. This proved to be a very demanding and difficult task, as Longstone was just bare rock only two metres above sea level. Massive blocks of granite were brought by sea from Yorkshire, and by February 1826 the magnificent circular tower, rising 26 metres above the sea, was completed.

Grace was ten years old when the family moved across from Brownsman to live on the bleak, more desolate and remote Longstone Island. Their home was the lighthouse. It had circular rooms with furniture built round the walls. The kitchen / living room was the largest room at the bottom of the tower, with three bedrooms rising above, each getting gradually smaller. They were reached by a winding staircase that continued on to a store room, then up to the lantern room at the very top, where the bright oil light with its revolving reflectors, flashed its white beam every twenty seconds. It was here in the lantern room that the children continued their lessons.

Although there were many advantages living in the new lighthouse, there were also disadvantages. There was much more work to do. The oil lamp had to be cleaned and filled regularly. The glass of the lamp had to be polished to keep the light bright and clear, and the windows of the lantern room, both inside and out, had to be kept clean. Also, as Longstone was just a bare rock it meant that every day they had to row back across to Brownsman to see to the animals and gather the fresh vegetables from the garden.

By 1834, the elder children had left the family home to live and work on the Mainland, but Grace and her younger brother William Brooks chose to stay on the Longstone to support and help their parents.

It was in 1838, when Grace was twenty two years old, that her name was written into our history books.

On the evening of the 5th of September 1838, the luxury steamship Forfarshire, the most splendid and powerful steam vessel, and one of the first ever cruise ships, left Hull bound for Dundee. It was carrying a cargo of fine material, soap and boiler plate, thirty nine passengers and a crew of twenty four. It had not travelled very far when one of its starboard boilers sprung a leak. Many of the passengers were very concerned and would rather have returned to Hull. The Captain, John Humble, after consultation with one of the engineers, who assured him that he had dealt with the problem by doing a temporary repair, decided to proceed.

Had the weather been favourable and the sea calm perhaps all would have been well, but as they sailed north the weather deteriorated and they ran into a terrible storm.

By 6.00pm the following evening the Forfarshire was passing the Farne Islands.

That same night Mr. and Mrs. Darling and Grace were the only three in the lighthouse. William Brooks had gone across to the village of Seahouses that morning to help his friends with the fishing, and because of the violence of the storm he had been unable to return home. Mr. and Mrs. Darling listened to the rain lashing against the windows, and the waves pounding and crashing against the lighthouse. The thunder cracked and the lightning lit up the room where they were sitting. Mr. Darling was afraid their coble would be dashed to pieces against the rocks. Never had he known a storm as ferocious as this. He roused Grace from her bed to help him secure their boat, and to bring inside things from the yard that might be blown away. They were soaked to the skin, as there were no oil skins or waterproof clothing of any kind in those days.

Having dried themselves by the fire, Mr. Darling went to bed, and Grace stayed with her mother to keep watch.

Meanwhile the Forfarshire was struggling northwards. Gale force winds and gigantic waves battered the ship and she was tossed about unmercifully. The leaking boiler could not be controlled and the engine room was awash with boiling water. Conditions were intolerable. At midnight as the Forfarshire reached St. Abb's Head, the engines failed and the ship began to drift south, driven by the violent winds. Captain Humble decided that he would try and reach the Inner Farne, the largest island, and take shelter until the storm had abated. Seeing a light in the distance he thought it was the Inner Farne light and tried to guide the ship around it. Sadly, in such appalling conditions he had made a mistake, for the light he had seen was the Longstone light.

At about 4.00am on the 7th of September 1838, the Forfarshire struck the Big Harcar rock and broke in two. Most of the passengers were below deck in their cabins unaware of the danger. Forty three people, including the captain and his wife, were cast into the sea and never seen again. Eight crew men and one young man, a passenger, managed to jump into a small lifeboat and by some miracle, the wind blew them away from the wreck and the islands and they were picked up the next day by another vessel.

Just after four thirty that morning Grace spotted the wreck from her bedroom window. She hurried down the stairs to tell her father, then together they went up to the top of the lighthouse and kept watch through their telescope. Because of the darkness and the spray being thrown up over the rocks they could not see any signs of life. It was not until seven o'clock that they spotted movement on the rocks. Immediately Grace pleaded with her father, "Please, we must go and help those poor souls, or they will surely die". Mr. Darling hesitated, not because he was afraid, for he had shown outstanding courage on many occasions, and rescued many shipwrecked sailors. In the past years he had had his sons to help him, but now there was only Grace. She had never been out in such treacherous seas, but he didn't doubt her courage. William did not think it would be possible for the Bamburgh lifeboat or the lifeboat from Seahouses to put out in such conditions.

He was sure they would be able to reach the wreck, but it would be impossible to return unless there were survivors who could help them as they would be rowing against the tide and against the storm.

Grace was impatient. She had no thought of danger or the risk to their own lives. She couldn't bear the thought of those poor people suffering or being washed into the sea. She was so determined, and said if her father wouldn't go with her she would go alone. Mr. Darling needed no persuading, and quickly they prepared themselves for the journey. Although Mrs. Darling begged them not to go, she helped them launch their coble, certain that she would never see them alive again. It was impossible to take the direct route to the wreck as they would have been exposed to the full fury of the storm and would most certainly have been dashed onto the rocks by the mountainous waves. Instead they went round the south side of the islands so they were sheltered most of way, though this meant they had to row twice the distance. As they approached the Big Harcar, they could see twelve people on the rock. The survivors were desperate to be rescued, but Mr. Darling knew it would be impossible to get them all into the coble in such conditions.

So as they drew close, he jumped out onto the rock, leaving Grace to hold the boat steady while he organised the survivors into two groups. How she had the strength to keep that coble, which usually took four people to row in such horrendous seas, from being broken to pieces on those jagged rocks is remarkable. Grace claimed that God was with her and gave her the strength she needed.

There were nine people still alive on the reef. There was one lady, Mrs. Dawson. She was holding in her arms the dead bodies of her two young children. There was also the dead body of a clergyman, the Revd. Mr. Robb. Mr. Darling helped Mrs. Dawson and an injured man into the boat along with three other men and they struggled back to the lighthouse. Grace remained there to help her mother look after the survivors while Mr. Darling made a second journey, with the assistance of two of the men they had rescued, who were both crewmen on the Forfarshire. Soon they were all safe in the lighthouse, four passengers and five members of the crew.

About two hours later William Brooks and six of his friends arrived at the lighthouse. At dawn the wreck of the Forfarshire had been spotted from Bamburgh Castle and a cannon had been fired to warn the lifeboats. However the lifeboat could not be launched from Seahouses but the three Robson brothers, William Brooks and two other fishermen set off in a fishing coble. When they reached the wreck two and a half hours later there were only the three dead bodies on the rocks. The seas being so wild it was impossible for them to get back to Seahouses, so they decided to take refuge in the lighthouse. The storm was so bad they all had to stay on the Longstone for two more days.

The Forfarshire, being the most luxurious, up-to-date vessel of its day, news of the wreck soon spread throughout the country, and when the survivors told of the young girl, who with her father, had rowed out and saved their lives, Grace soon became famous.

Her name was on everyone's lips. Glowing reports of her appeared in newspapers telling of her heroic deed. People wrote asking for locks of her hair. Artists arrived on the island to paint her portrait, poets to write verse and boat trips were organised just to take people out to look at her. Gifts were showered on her, offers of marriage were made and she was even invited to appear on the stage in London.

The Royal Humane Society awarded Grace and her father their Honorary Gold Medal, and the Royal National Institution for the Preservation of Life from Shipwreck awarded them both Silver Medals. Gifts of money were sent and a fund was set up for Grace in recognition of her heroic deed. Queen Victoria herself donated £50 to the fund. However Grace had very little from the money. Most of it was held in trust. The Duke of Northumberland, who knew the family well, became Grace's guardian, to shelter her from all the publicity.

Grace hated all the fuss. She always claimed she had done nothing outstanding, only doing her Christian duty. She continued to live at the lighthouse but life was never the same. The peace and tranquility had gone. There was always somebody coming to pry and ask questions.

The Silver Medals were awarded to Grace and her Father by the Royal Institution for the Preservation of Life from Shipwreck. This was the forerunner of the Royal National Lifeboat Institution (R.N.L.I.)

Not long after the event Grace developed a nasty cough. At first it did not seem to cause much concern, but the cough persisted. It was tuberculosis. Her parents decided that she needed a rest, and she was sent to stay with friends in Wooler. However her condition worsened and she went to stay with a cousin in Alnwick where she was attended by the Duke of Northumberland's physician. Grace longed to go home to be by the sea she loved. Her sister Thomasin took Grace home to Bamburgh, and it was there, in Thomasin's cottage, on the 20th of October 1842, at the age of twenty six that Grace died. She was buried in St. Aidan's Churchyard directly opposite her grandfather's cottage where she was born.

Her great courage and her modesty were a shining example to everyone. People wished that she would always be remembered and money was raised to build a monument in her memory. There it stands to this day, in a prominent position where it can be seen from the sea, and hundreds of people, both young and old come to the churchyard every year to pay their respects to a young, courageous girl called Grace Darling, who risked her life to save others.

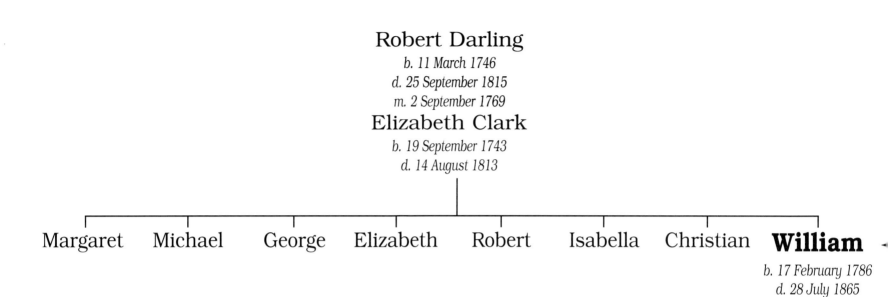

Robert Darling
b. 11 March 1746
d. 25 September 1815
m. 2 September 1769

Elizabeth Clark
b. 19 September 1743
d. 14 August 1813

Margaret   Michael   George   Elizabeth   Robert   Isabella   Christian   **William**

William
b. 17 February 1786
d. 28 July 1865
Married

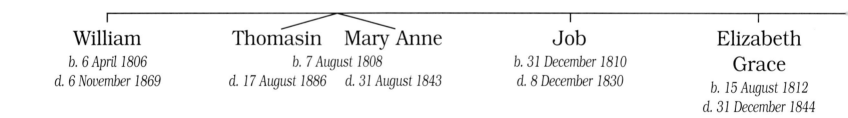

William
b. 6 April 1806
d. 6 November 1869

Thomasin   Mary Anne
b. 7 August 1808
d. 17 August 1886   *d. 31 August 1843*

Job
b. 31 December 1810
d. 8 December 1830

Elizabeth
Grace
b. 15 August 1812
d. 31 December 1844

Family Tree (fuller version available from the Grace Darling Museum, Bamburgh)

Job Horsley
b. 22 November 1733
d. 26 March 1826
m. 1773

Grace Watson
b. 1742
d. March 1814

| **Thomasin** | Grace | Elizabeth | Alexander | Mary Reed | George Reed Horsley | Margaret | Robert |

Thomasin
b.27 February 1774
d. 16 October 1848

1st July 1805

Robert
b. March 1814
d. 1877

GRACE HORSLEY DARLING
b. 24 November 1815
d. 20 October 1842

George Alexander
b. 14 August 1819
d. 20 April 1903

William Brooks
d. December 1870

*After Grace's death, the public raised money to build this beautiful memorial which stands in
St. Aidan's Church Yard, where it can also be seen from the sea by passing ships.*